Eastman Johnson

Eastman Johnson

BY PATRICIA HILLS

 CLARKSON N. POTTER, INC. / PUBLISHER   NEW YORK

IN ASSOCIATION WITH THE WHITNEY MUSEUM OF AMERICAN ART

DISTRIBUTED BY CROWN PUBLISHERS, INC.

Frontispiece: *Self-Portrait.* (1859). Oil on canvas.
30¼ x 27⅞ inches. National Academy of Design.
This self-portrait was done the year he was made
an Associate of the National Academy.

Printed in the United States of America
Library of Congress Catalog Card Number: 70–186696
Published simultaneously in Canada by General Publishing Company Limited.

Inquiries should be addressed to Clarkson N. Potter,
Inc., 419 Park Avenue South, New York, N.Y. 10016.
First Edition

Acknowledgments

I want especially to thank the following, whose continuing enthusiasm for my research on Eastman Johnson has been most supportive: Stuart P. Feld, John K. Howat, Ken Lux, James Pilgrim, Theodore E. Stebbins, Jr., and Leo Steinberg. Others have directed me to Johnson paintings and research resources which I otherwise would not have known, and to them I am grateful: Peter Davidson, Colin Eisler, M. Roy Fisher, Lawrence A. Fleischman, Alfred Frankenstein, William H. Gerdts, Mrs. Barbara Groseclose, Francis S. Grubar, Graham Hood, Mrs. McCook Knox, Cecily Langdale, Alice Melrose, Maria Naylor, Clyde Newhouse, Thomas Norton, Helmut Ripperger, Ira Spanierman, Natalie Spassky, Roger B. Stein, Robert C. Vose, Jr., H. Wade White, and John Wilmerding. The staffs of the New York office of the Archives of American Art, the Frick Art Reference Library, the New-York Historical Society, the New York Public Library Art Reference Room, and the St. Louis County Historical Society of Duluth have been unfailingly helpful and most patient with all my inquiries. I also want to acknowledge Jeanne Hamilton who printed photographs when I needed them.

I want to thank the Danforth Foundation and its Director of Graduate Fellowships for Women, Miss Mary Brucker, for grants which enabled me to pursue my studies at the Institute of Fine Arts of New York University and to travel to do research in several cities within the United States.

The living relatives of Eastman Johnson have been most helpful by supplying me with biographical information and permitting me to read family papers. My research was greatly facilitated by the many private collectors who invited me to see the paintings and drawings by Johnson in their homes.

I wish further to acknowledge John Walsh, Jr., who gave me many constructive suggestions in the early drafts of the manuscript. Robert Goldwater helped to clarify several ideas at critical points in my manuscript, and I am most grateful for his guidance. My special thanks are due my husband, Frederic Hills, who contributed useful editorial suggestions at all stages.

Finally, I appreciate the encouragement of John Baur from the inception of my research on Johnson in 1968 to the final reading of the manuscript; his continuing support in all phases of the project has been invaluable.

Eastman Johnson

Preface

Highly regarded in America's Victorian age by artists and public alike, Eastman Johnson fell into oblivion in the early years of the twentieth century, when his works were considered old-fashioned. In 1920 an exhibition of his drawings, held at the galleries of Kennedy and Company, turned the attention of many collectors toward Johnson. But it was not until the late 1930s that interest in his work was again revived, first by a small exhibition organized by Norman Hirschl at the Frazier Gallery in 1937 and then by the large Johnson exhibition organized by John I. H. Baur for the Brooklyn Museum in 1940. Baur's selection struck a balance between the popular favorites of Johnson's time and the private sketches which Johnson had given to friends or had kept in his studio until the end of his life.

The Johnson paintings met with a mixed reception from the critics of the early forties. The private sketches were greeted with enthusiasm, while the finished, often sentimental, works were received with embarrassment. Johnson, it was declared, was definitely not a Homer or an Eakins. In subsequent accounts of the period, this critical comparison has persisted without acknowledging that Johnson was twelve years older than Homer and twenty years older than Eakins, and hence his experience of life and his concerns about art were fundamentally different. That Johnson could and did paint pictures which urge a sentimental rather than an aesthetic response reflects the attitude of a generation for whom "right sentiment" was still the most important criterion of "ideal art."

Nor does the criticism that praises the sketches and condemns the lack of spontaneity of the finished works acknowledge that to academically oriented painters of Johnson's generation, the sketch was an integral part of the process by which one arrived at the finished work. If we do incline toward Johnson's sketches, we should be aware that that preference has, in part, been fostered by the aesthetic beliefs of the artists following Johnson's generation. A radical break occurred when Manet and the Impressionists insisted that a spontaneous impression of a subject is more truthful to nature than a subsequent, highly finished, studio-rendered work. They insisted upon this point because, as avowed realists, they believed that truthfulness to nature rather than right sentiment satisfied the prime requirement of art. To adherents of such an artistic philosophy, the finished studio work was not just superfluous but contemptibly artificial.

We have evidence that Johnson, too, privately delighted in his first sketches and he kept them on the walls of his studio for years, but he was reluctant to exhibit them as "works of art." To Johnson, who belonged both in chronology and in philosophy to an earlier generation than the Impressionists, the sketches were preliminary—a means to an end.

In the last few years, nineteenth-century art has been undergoing a reassessment. Essays which outlined the stylistic developments of a handful of innovative geniuses who soared above their less talented contemporaries have been supplemented by scholarly investigations into the contributions of minor painters, official and private patronage, the methods of academic instruction, and the choice and nature of the pictorial themes. We now recognize that significant, indigenous art does not spring forth from its own unique artistic impulse (although, indeed, that may seem to account for the difference between major and minor artists), but must be understood as it evolves out of the rich detail and pattern of an entire culture. We must also recognize that the particular flavor of American art is more successfully elucidated in studies that draw parallels between American and European developments than in those studies that treat our art as if it had developed in a national vacuum, uninfluenced by European art and culture.

The present essay should be considered a companion to John Baur's study of Johnson in the Brooklyn Museum catalogue of 1940, to which all students of the artist are deeply indebted. This essay, then, emphasizes the artistic and cultural forces which shaped the work of Johnson, investigates the sources—both European and American—and development of his style and themes, and attempts to define Johnson's place in the art and life of our country.*

*The specific paintings cited in the text but not illustrated are followed by the names of their owners enclosed in parentheses.

4

Eastman Johnson

Eastman Johnson (1824–1906) began his artistic career in the mid-1840s as a crayon limner of his New England neighbors and ended it at his death as the portrait painter of late nineteenth-century American presidents, industrialists, financiers, and wealthy professional men. In the intervening years—from the mid-fifties to the mid-eighties—he marshaled his main creative energies and preoccupations for the depiction of scenes of everyday life. His attraction to that branch of painting termed "genre," the nature of the scenes depicted, the styles in which he worked, and his eventual shift away from such scenes are all intimately related to the artistic aims and aspirations of the painters of his time and to the needs and demands of changing public taste.

Johnson understood and shared in the sensibilities of his time. His personality, as revealed in his letters and evoked by the comments of his colleagues, embodied the conventional virtues of his age: he was a pragmatic, tactful man, sympathetic to the tribulations of his friends, chivalrous with women, and fond of children. His sense of humor was broad and light, even at times sentimental.

But his powers as a genre painter, sharpened by European training, were, in the early 1860s, unrivaled. When elected as an Associate to the National Academy of Design in 1859, he was recognized as the most talented young painter of American domestic life in New York. Throughout the 1860s and the 1870s he sustained his skill in infusing fresh life into old themes and discovered subjects to which he gave a new dignity and a new content. When he gave up genre themes in the 1880s, he had already left behind a body of work that assured his place in history.

EARLY WORKS AND EUROPEAN SOJOURN

Born in Lovell, Maine, on July 29, 1824, Jonathan Eastman Johnson grew up in Fryeburg and later Augusta, Maine, where his father held various positions in the state government. Learning to draw while still in high school, he proved amazingly talented as a draftsman. After a brief stint as a clerk in a dry goods store, where he displayed no bent for business, his father sent him to a lithography shop in Boston to learn the lithographer's trade. By 1842 young Eastman was back in Augusta doing crayon portraits of his family, his friends, and his father's business associates.

Head of a Woman. July 1844. Charcoal and chalk on paper, 13½ x 10⅝ inches. The Brooklyn Museum, Carll H. DeSilver Fund.

Head of a Man. July 1844. Charcoal and chalk on paper, 12¾ x 10¾ inches. The Brooklyn Museum, Carll H. DeSilver Fund.

Head of a Man and *Head of a Woman,* done in July 1844, when Johnson was just turning twenty, are the earliest located examples of his work. There is, in both, an unidealized frankness and an emphasis on the lineaments of age that lead us to suppose that the drawings were good likenesses, a criterion of paramount importance to Yankee patrons since the days of the early limners. They are, however, clearly by the hand of one untrained in the subtleties of academic methods. Light and shadow operate not to unify the form but solely to clarify each individual feature.

Johnson seems to have made a modest income with his crayon portraits, traveling to local towns to find commissions, and passing several months in Portland, Maine. But the pivotal moment in his career came sometime in late 1844 or 1845 when Johnson decided to move to Washington, D.C., in order to establish himself in the portrait business. Johnson was permitted, perhaps through his father's political connections, to occupy one of the Senate committee rooms as a studio. It was Johnson's avowed ambition to gather for himself a portfolio of drawings of eminent Americans, and to this end many of the capital's most distinguished citizens obliged him with sittings. Among those who sat for this extraordinary young

Left: *John Quincy Adams.* (April 1, 1846). Pencil and crayon on paper, 21½ x 15½ inches. Private collection. Photograph courtesy M. Knoedler & Co., Inc. John Quincy Adams recorded in his diary that he posed for Johnson for one hour on April 1, 1846, in one of the committee rooms in the House of Representatives. Right: *Dolley Madison.* March 1846. Crayon heightened with white on paper, 21¼ x 14¾ inches. Fogg Art Museum, Harvard University, gift of Grenville L. Winthrop.

man of twenty-two were judges of the Supreme Court, John Quincy Adams, Daniel Webster, Dolley Madison, and Mrs. Alexander Hamilton.

For his portraits of John Quincy Adams and Dolley Madison, Johnson attempted an ambitious composition with all of the background filled in with pencil and charcoal. The Adams portrait is unfinished, perhaps because Johnson felt he needed another sitting, but it indicates his technique. Although the background, hands, coat, and shirt are summarily sketched, Adams's head is solidly sculpted and his features are clearly delineated. In the portrait of *Dolley Madison,* Johnson provided the finishing touches to the portrait by adding details of femininity, highlights to enliven the surface, and intermediate halftones to smooth out the modeling of the face. The portrait of *Mrs. Alexander Hamilton* appears to have been quickly sketched, and the spontaneity of the technique suggests an analogous spontaneity of personality of the sitter.

Mrs. Alexander Hamilton. March 1846. Crayon, pencil and chalk on paper, 14¾ x 12¾ inches. The New-York Historical Society.

During 1846 Johnson's popularity as a portrait draftsman grew enormously. Henry Wadsworth Long-fellow persuaded him to come to Boston and engaged him to draw the portraits of his family and literary friends. These portraits included those of Ralph Waldo Emerson, Nathaniel Hawthorne, Charles Sumner, and Longfellow himself, all of which were executed first with charcoal and then finished with hard crayons, the modeling being filled in with a stump.[1] As his lifelong friend the painter George H. Hall later recalled, Johnson at this time worked rapidly and with a sure hand, seldom finding it necessary to make corrections; his drawings never took more than two or three sittings and were often finished in one day.[2]

As a young man working among distinguished figures, Johnson undoubtedly assimilated some of the literary ideas current in Longfellow's and Emerson's circle. New England transcendentalism, which had revealed itself in the pages of *The Dial* in the early 1840s, would not have appealed to him, a man of sense and practicality. Rather it was Emerson's and Longfellow's preoccupation with the notion of an indigenously "American" literature that would have struck a sympathetic chord in the artist. Emerson, who reportedly had impressed the young Johnson, had scolded his countrymen: "We have listened too long to the courtly muses of Europe."[3] And he urged poets and artists to turn to local subject matter:

We have yet had no genius in America with tyrannous eye, which knew the value of our incomparable materials. ... Our logrolling, our stumps, and their politics, our fisheries, our Negros and Indians, our boats ... the northern trade, the southern planting, the western clearing, Oregon and Texas, are yet unsung. Yet America is a poem in our eyes; its ample geography dazzles the imagination.[4]

Ralph Waldo Emerson. Circa October 22, 1846. Crayon and chalk, 21 x 19 inches oval. Longfellow House Trust.

These and similar exhortations must have lingered in Johnson's mind, and in the late 1850s he was to take up their challenge.

Johnson progressed to pastels while in Boston and most likely experimented with oils, but by the summer of 1849 he had resolved to go to Europe with his friend George Hall to seek art instruction unavailable in this country and to study at first hand the old masters. They were coaxed into choosing Düsseldorf rather than another art center in Europe by the American Art-Union,[5] the most important organ of artistic patronage in America in the 1840s. Hall had wanted to study in Italy, but Andrew Warner, Corresponding Secretary for the Union, advised:

Before you fully determine on taking up your residence in Italy in the prosecution of your studies I would advise that you should see the Düsseldorf Collection in this City. These German paintings show great knowledge of the art. It is thought that better opportunities for a student in painting are offered in Germany than in Italy at this time....Mr. Leutze you are aware is a resident at Düsseldorf, and has made astonishing progress in his profession there, and he would doubtless be happy to afford every encouragement in his power to a fellow countryman going out there for such objects as yours.[6]

The Düsseldorf Gallery in New York, a gallery of some fifty-six paintings gathered by John G. Boker, had just opened the previous January, and the style of the Düsseldorf School was considered the modern, advanced style of painting in New York. What was most admired were the technical abilities of the German masters—abilities that were recognized as sorely wanting among American painters because of the lack of adequate training facilities in America. Moreover, the Düsseldorf School was known above all as a genre school. And the American Art-Union was anxious to have artists not only well trained but trained specifically in the field of genre. Genre paintings made their primary appeal to human sentiment rather than to the aesthetic faculties and thus were easily understood and popular among the majority of the subscribers to the Art-Union.

Hall and Johnson let themselves be persuaded by the Art-Union; on July 24, 1849, Hall wrote to Mr. Warner:

I am very much obliged to you for your kindness in making the inquiries concerning Düsseldorf. Mr. Johnson and myself have decided that the Academy is the best place for us, and we shall be ready about the fifteenth of August for our departure....[7]

Thus, in mid-August of 1849, the two young men sailed to Düsseldorf with high hopes and the blessing of the American Art-Union.

After spending a week or two in Holland, Johnson and his friend Hall went on to Düsseldorf, where Johnson attended classes at the Royal Academy,[8] whose well-known teachers then included Karl Friedrich Lessing, Andreas Achenbach, and the director, Wilhelm von Schadow. The beginning student was expected to demonstrate a mastery of drawing from the cast and figure before being admitted to the painting classes, and for most students this meant spending months and even years before they were allowed to handle a brush. Johnson attended a class in anatomical drawing in the fall, but no available records reveal exactly when he began taking classes in painting. He made at least some progress in oil by October 1850 when he sent two works to the American Art-Union for sale. However, in a letter accompanying the shipment his admission that he was sending the pictures "rather earlier in my practice of oils than I should otherwise do" would indicate that he had not been painting long.[9] The oils, *Peasants of the Rhine* and *The Junior Partner,* have long since disappeared; all that can be surmised is that they were the efforts of a self-proclaimed beginner.

The several very fine drawings which still exist from this period show an advance, in academic terms, over the drawings done in America. A comparison between the *Portrait of a Young Man* of 1848 and *Langhamer,* dated November 1849, illustrates his progress. The later drawing exhibits a lighter touch; the features do not stand out as isolated units. The path of the crayon travels over the contours of the face and unites all the elements into a single, forceful image; the eyes seem to rest in the depths of their sockets and the eyebrows appear to grow organically from the protruding bony ridge. Moreover, the later drawing suggests that Johnson was consciously attempting to be more "artful," to do more than merely render the sitter's facial topography. There is a certain romantic dash to the young man's glance, to his tousled hair, and to the swirling patterns of his beard.

In January 1851 Johnson entered the studio of Emanuel Leutze, the most renowned of the Americans in Düsseldorf, and found the artistic atmosphere congenial. He wrote to the American Art-Union of his enthusiasm for Leutze:

I have now recently gone with Mr. Leutze and am painting under his instruction in an immense atelier which he rented for his big picture [*George Washington Crossing the Delaware*], with others beside himself, excellent artists, and both engaged on large works, forming an atmosphere and an aspect of art not less delightful than it is improving, and I regret now that I had not been with him during my entire stay in Düsseldorf.[10]

The first version of Leutze's *Washington Crossing the Delaware* (destroyed during World War II) had been damaged by fire the previous November. Leutze was about to begin a second version (Metropolitan Museum of Art, New York) when an agent of Goupil, Vibert and Company, the large Paris firm of art dealers and publishers, arrived to purchase the painting. In 1849 the New York branch of Goupil had established the profit-making "International Art-Union" in competition with the nonprofit American Art-Union, and the French firm now planned to exhibit Leutze's painting throughout the United States. Johnson tried unsuccessfully to intercede on behalf of the nonprofit American Art-Union, which, because of their steadfast support of American art, he thought deserved an option. Later in the winter Johnson copied the painting in a reduced size for Goupil's engraver Paul Girardet.[11]

After a brief trip to Holland and to London in the summer of 1851 to see the International Exposition, Johnson resolved to leave his Düsseldorf friends and move to The Hague where he could study the Dutch masters at first hand. A letter of November 20, 1851, to the American Art-Union articulates his final dissatisfaction with the Düsseldorf school:

Portrait of a Young Man. 1848. Charcoal and crayon on paper, 18 x 15 inches oval. IBM Corporation. This portrait may well be a self-portrait.

Langhamer. November 1849. Charcoal on paper, 23¾ x 18¾ inches. Museum of Fine Arts, Boston, M. and M. Karolik Collection.

Head of a Woman. Circa 1849. Charcoal on paper, 14 x 16 inches. Collection of Rita and Daniel Fraad.

Andreas Achenbach. June 1851. Pencil on paper, 7½ x
8¼ inches. Collection of Mr. and Mrs. Theodore E.
Stebbins, Jr. Andreas Achenbach was one of the instruc-
tors at the Royal Academy of Düsseldorf during the time
that Johnson was staying there.

I am at present... at the Hague, where I find I am deriving much advantage from studying the splendid works
of Rembrandt and a few other of the old Dutch masters, who I find are only to be seen in Holland. I shall
probably continue here a good portion of the winter. I must say I regret having spent so long a time in
Düsseldorf when there is nothing to see but the present artists, who, whatever their merits may be, are very
deficient in some of the chief requisites, as in color, in which they are certainly scarcely tolerable. Leutze was the
only colorist amongst them....[12]

Johnson stayed on in Holland much longer than just the winter, however, and made copies after
Van Dyck's *Anna Wake, Lady Sheffield* (whereabouts unknown) and a detail of Rembrandt's *The
Anatomy Lesson* (whereabouts unknown).

The subjects he now chose for his compositions were those that had been popular in the Dutch genre
tradition since the seventeenth century. The robed and turbaned figure in the drawing *Study of an Oriental*
recalls Rembrandt's studies of men dressed in fanciful Middle Eastern costumes (compare, for example,

14

Study of an Oriental. Circa 1851-1855. Pencil on paper, 21¼ x 15 inches. Museum of Fine Arts, Boston, M. and M. Karolik Collection.

The Counterfeiters. Circa 1851-1855. Oil on canvas, 29½ x 36½ inches. IBM Corporation.

The Noble Slav, Metropolitan Museum of Art, New York). The drawing reveals Johnson's mastery of nineteenth-century European academic techniques; a delicate, pencil chiaroscuro models the face and hands and a clean outline circumscribes the bulk of the figure. The depiction of rogues, such as those in *The Counterfeiters* and cardsharps and their unwitting dupes, as in *The Card Players,* had amused Dutch patrons since the time of Honthorst, Terbrugghen, and other Dutch followers of Caravaggio. With *The Counterfeiters,* set in a Dutch courtyard, Johnson attempted a scene of melodramatic action, in which light is used to dramatize the narrative. The shaft of light entering from the left suggests an outside presence about to discover the clandestine crime. The figures, however, do not coalesce into a coherent image, and Johnson left the painting unfinished. Better suited to his talents at this time were shallow-spaced tableaus, such as *The Card Players* with its picturesque cast of gamblers, an old toothless grandfather, and a little girl urging her elderly friend home. The surface of the canvas is uniformly finished with an eye for realism of detail. Here light functions to reveal the various textures and local color of the *trompe l'oeil* details—the grandfather's fur hat, the open drawer, the pipe and cup, the tattered book, the clock, the slate and the curtains, to name only a few—details which compete with the anecdote for our attention. *The Savoyard Boy,* with its idealized young worker, has no anecdote; here the figure holds its own against a backdrop of rusticated wall and vines and leaves—a picturesque backdrop Johnson used in several paintings of this period.

With the help and sponsorship of August Belmont, then the American ambassador to The Hague, Johnson also carved out a lucrative career for himself as a portraitist. Johnson executed portraits of Mrs. Belmont, her son Perry, their friends, and several ladies of the court. The drawings of women, such as the charcoal study of Polly Gary (Deerfield Academy), are delicate and proficient. The portraits of children, however, tend to be overly pretty and sweet, perhaps in response to the expectations of the patrons and contemporary convention.

His most notable oil portrait of this time was of Worthington Whittredge, which he painted during a visit to Düsseldorf in 1854. This likeness of his lifelong friend indicates his mastery of oil portraiture and his indebtedness to Rembrandt and seventeenth-century Dutch portrait painting. The face with its smooth, ivory flesh tones emerging out of deep shadowed areas possesses at once a dignity and a sense of mystery.

According to William Walton, who wrote a brief biography of Johnson shortly after the latter's death, Johnson was held in such high esteem that he was offered the position of court painter toward the end of his stay in Holland.[13] While this would have been an appropriate post for the young Johnson, who could oblige his subjects with a pleasing likeness and yet retain a freshness of approach, he declined the position. He felt the need for further study, and in the late summer of 1855 he moved to Paris, where many of his former friends, such as G. P. A. Healy and the German painter Ludwig Knaus, had moved, and where Thomas Hicks, E. Wood Perry, and others had already gravitated to the studio of Thomas Couture.[14] Couture was a revelation to young American painters in Paris. He was more accessible than the teachers at the École des Beaux-Arts, he took great interest in his American students, and he taught prescriptively, with an emphasis on method. To Americans, *method* was the elixir lacking in America and found only in Europe.

The Card Players. 1853. Oil on canvas, 21 x 27¾ inches sight. Private collection.

Opposite: *The Savoyard Boy.* 1853. Oil on canvas, 37⅜ x 32¼ inches. The Brooklyn Museum, bequest of Henry P. Martin.

19

At the time of Johnson's arrival, Couture was working on several commissions for murals; Johnson reportedly made a copy of a head of a sleeping soldier after Couture. He seems to have thrived under Couture's influence, but his stay was cut short by news of his mother's death.[15] In late October he returned home to America, having had an eclectic training that combined Düsseldorf, Dutch old master, and French influences.

Worthington Whittredge. 1854. Oil on canvas, 37 x 26¼ inches.
The Detroit Institute of Arts, Dexter M. Ferry, Jr., Fund.

Secretary Dobbin. 1856. Charcoal and chalk on paper, 27 x 19 inches. Addison Gallery of American Art, Phillips Academy, Andover, Massachusetts. James Cochrane Dobbin was Secretary of the Navy under President Pierce.

RETURN TO AMERICA

Johnson went directly to Washington, taking with him some of the paintings he had done in Europe. Two of these paintings, *The Card Players* and *The Savoyard,* were exhibited at the National Academy of Design in the spring of 1856.[16]

In the summer of 1856 he visited his sister Sarah and her husband in Superior, Wisconsin. To Johnson, who had not yet established a career for himself in Washington, the trip to the Duluth area gave him a chance to see the American frontier. While there, he invested in land and painted several portraits.

He was back in Washington, however, in the spring of 1857, and exploring new subjects to paint. He had gone to Europe not to improve his portrait style but to master figure and genre compositions.

Moreover, portrait drawings in the 1850s were being superseded by daguerreotypes, a novel medium which satisfied the public's need for informal portraits. The alternatives open to him in genre were to look for new subjects or to continue in the tradition of William Sidney Mount, whose anecdotal rustic scenes had proved so popular with the art public in the 1840s and 1850s. In either case, the cultural pressure to select themes that were "American" was great. In the writings of his colleagues and critics of the time, the need to portray the American scene and its people constituted a kind of national artistic imperative.[17]

A uniquely American subject awaited Johnson in Washington—the old Washington mansion at Mount Vernon that was in desperate need of restoration. Johnson painted an undistinguished view of the house and its grounds in 1857 (collection Sons of the Revolution). Landscape painting was not Johnson's forte, and few of his landscapes exist that carry any special stamp of their authorship.

A notable step forward in his career came with his return to Duluth in the summer of 1857, where he became fascinated with the Chippewa Indians living in the area. He traveled 150 miles to one of their camps at Grand Portage, where he lived for several months, sketching them in their native setting.

Grand Portage. (1857). Oil on canvas, 9 x 19½ inches. St. Louis County Historical Society, Duluth.

22

Canoe of Indians. (1857). Oil on canvas, 17¾ x 38¾ inches. St. Louis County Historical Society, Duluth.

In turning to Indians as a source of subject matter, he was, of course, following in the path of many European artists who had been fascinated by and had represented the New World inhabitants since shortly after the voyage of Columbus. In the intervening centuries, the Indians had been reduced to a number of stock stereotypes—being represented in art as well as literature as noble savages, as brutal heathens, or as carefree, irresponsible wards of the white man. However, after the Secretary of War in 1824 declared that the Indians as a race were approaching extinction, artists responded by hastening to paint what seemed to be the last generation of Indians. The government commissioned portraits of the Indian chiefs by Charles Bird King and James Otto Lewis[18]; other artists intent on recording the picturesque surface of Indian life, such as George Catlin and Karl Bodmer, made precise drawings and paintings of their dress, headgear, weapons, and domestic utensils. The popular literature of the period abounded in stories of the "Last Indian"—the dispossessed Noble Savage who had to step aside and had to die because of the exigencies of civilization and the demands of "manifest destiny." It was a situation not unlike that of Lewis Carroll's Walrus, who weeps over the helpless oysters while gorging himself on them.

Certainly such cultural currents affected Johnson's decision to paint Indians. Among the influences that would have been most relevant to his study of the Chippewas was Longfellow's *Hiawatha,* published in 1855, a popular epic poem which closely followed Schoolcraft's version of a cycle of Chippewa legends.[19] Moreover, in the January 1856 issue of *The Crayon,* a widely read art magazine, appeared an editorial, "The Indians in American Art." This editorial formulated what was, in effect, an artistic program for Johnson and many other painters.

It seems to us that the Indian has not received justice in American art.... It should be held in dutiful remembrance that he is fast passing away from the face of the earth. Soon the last red man will have faded forever from his native land, and those who come after us will trust to our scanty records for their knowledge of his habits and appearance.... Absorbed in his quiet dignity, brave, honest, eminently truthful, and always thoroughly in earnest, he stands grandly apart from all other known savage life. As such, let him be, for justice sake, sometimes represented.[20]

Johnson's paintings include two small distant views of the camp at Grand Portage, closeup views of teepees, groups of Indians standing, sitting, and riding in a canoe, and single figures. No attempt has been made to compose the figures into well-ordered dramatic groupings. Johnson's intention seems to have been to record on paper and on canvas information about the physiognomy, costumes, and environment of the Indians with little dramatic or sentimental editorializing. But in the studies of the heads, particularly those done in crayon and charcoal, Johnson has gone beyond mere factual reportage and has given us portraits of a dignified and proud people. The features of these Indians, the high cheekbones, dark eyes, strong noses, and thick black hair, are striking. Although the visages seem idealized, they represent specific people whose Indian names are inscribed next to their portraits: Kenne wa be mint, Kay be sen dey way We win, Sha wen Negun, Mados way beek, and Wigemar wasung. Johnson kept these drawings and paintings for himself, and although he showed them to his friends, he never exhibited them during his lifetime. His contemporary, the art critic Henry Tuckerman, an unrelenting advocate of the depiction of American life, praised them in his *Book of the Artists* of 1867 and voiced his hope that Johnson would continue these subjects:

In a few years the Indian traits will grow vague; and never yet have they been adequately represented in Art. Catlin's aboriginal portraits are indeed valuable and authentic; Ward's statue of the Indian Hunter, and Crawford's of the Indian in his conscience [sic] decadence, are beautiful memorials, but much remains to be done in pictorial art. A recent glance into the portfolio of Eastman Johnson convinced us that he would do peculiar justice to a comparatively unworked mine of native art.... We have never seen the savage melancholy, the resigned stoicism, or the weird age of the American Indian, so truly portrayed: a Roman profile here, a fierce sadness there, a grim, withered physiognomy, or a soft but subdued wild beauty, prove how the artist's eye had caught the individuality of the aboriginal face; and with the picturesque costume, to imagine what an effective representative picture of the Red Man of America, with adequate facilities, this artist could execute.[21]

Double Head Study—Indians. (1857). Oil on canvas, 7 x 11½ inches. St. Louis County Historical Society, Duluth.

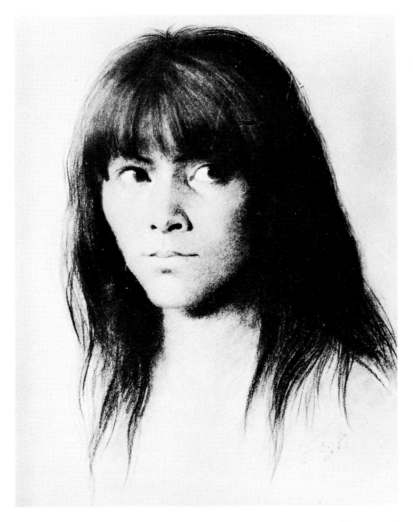

Indian Head. October 1857. Charcoal and crayon on paper, 16¾ x 13½ inches. St. Louis County Historical Society, Duluth.

Indian Profile. (1857). Charcoal, crayon and pencil on paper, 7 x 6½ inches. St. Louis County Historical Society, Duluth.

Life in the South. 1859. Oil on canvas, 36 x 45 inches. The New-York Historical Society. The original title given to the painting when it was exhibited at the National Academy of Design in 1859 was *Negro Life at the South*. By 1867, it was known as "Old Kentucky Home," a name adopted from Stephen Foster's popular song.

Southern Courtship. 1859. Oil on canvas, 20 x 15¾ inches. Collection of Ambassador and Mrs. J. William Middendorf II, New York. This is one of several paintings that Johnson did after parts of *Life in the South.*

In terms of quality, these studies are among the outstanding examples of Indians in art in the nine-teenth century. Although Johnson painted Indian domestic scenes when he visited Murray Bay, Canada, in the summer of 1869, he never again devoted such care to the portrayal of individual Indians.[22]

Toward the end of 1857 Johnson moved on to Cincinnati where he did several portraits, but by April 1858 he was in New York City, where he took a studio in the University Building on Washington Square. In the summer he returned to scenes of Mount Vernon, finishing a fanciful painting of the tomb of Wash-ington and an interior of the rustic kitchen.

In 1858 he probably also began work on *Life in the South*,[23] which, when it was exhibited in April 1859 at the National Academy of Design Annual Exhibition, was widely praised by critics and public alike. It was the painting that established Johnson's reputation and assured his election as an Associate Academician, an honor that was invaluable in securing an artist's fortune. The painting has become today, perhaps unjustly, the picture by which Johnson is best known and the one most frequently cited to illustrate all of the artist's worst faults.

We must remember that in 1859 *Life in the South* was considered one of the best genre paintings done by an American to date. Johnson had returned from Europe with his lessons well learned: the figures were well proportioned; the colors were distributed with finesse; and the composition was balanced. To a mid-century American, the general dilapidation of the slave quarters was picturesque, and the small anecdotal touches were delightful. The cumulative effect was one of correct sentiment justly expressed.

An anonymous critic for the June 1859 issue of the *Cosmopolitan Art Journal,* who had voiced his disappointment with the exhibition at the National Academy that year, singled out Johnson's painting for praise:

Out of this very large catalogue not to exceed 20 can be called pictures of the second class—of the first-class works there is not a single one, except it be Mr. Johnson's "Southern Life," which we are disposed to regard as, in several respects, a first-class character piece.[24]

Writing at length about the painting in the June issue of *The Crayon,* another reviewer began with the acknowledgment that exhibitions invariably reflect the public taste of the time and that painters who wish to be exhibited are obliged to cater to that taste. The reviewer's awareness of the dependence of artists on the often unsophisticated and often ambivalent aesthetic attitudes of their public is unusual for the time.

Exhibitions do not display the merits of particular works of Art and the progress of individual artists so much as they do the nature of public taste, or rather the character of artistic thought which the public chooses to manifest through its encouragement of Art.... It is a mistake to suppose that artists are free to paint what pleases them best.... The truth is, that artists are compelled to meet the public by consulting its likes and dislikes.[25]

The reviewer's discussion of the painting, however, is notable less for its astuteness than for its representativeness:

Negro Boy. (1860). Oil on canvas, 14 x 17⅛ inches. National Academy of Design. Johnson gave this small painting to the National Academy when he was elected a full Academician.

One of the best pictures in respect to Art and the most popular, because presenting familiar aspects of life, is E. Johnson's "Negro Life at the South." Here are several groups of negroes, who are assembled in the rear of a dilapidated house.... Although a very humble subject, this picture is a very instructive one in relation to Art. It is conscientously studied and painted, and full of ideas. Notwithstanding the general ugliness of the forms and objects, we recognize that its sentiment is one of beauty, for imitation and expression are vitalized by conveying to our mind the enjoyment of human beings in new and vivid aspects. We speak of the picture at length, because the Art by which the *beauty* of the subject is conveyed to our minds is of the most excellent description. The picture of "Negro Life at the South" ranks with Wilkie's "Blind Fiddler," and is a kind of Art that will be always popular, so long as lowly life exists to excite and to reveal the play of human sympathy.[26]

In terms of style *Life in the South* owes its greatest debt to contemporary European painting. The minuteness of detail, the relatively small scale of the figures, the blending of dry brushstrokes, and the deployment of local colors in an arbitrary but picturesque array certainly reflects a Düsseldorf training. The handling of the paint in the foreground, however, suggests Couture's technique of finishing off a painting with quick strokes of a loaded brush—thus achieving the effect of effortlessness. As in the "panorama" scenes that enjoyed such a vogue both in Europe and America in the first half of the nineteenth century, there are multiple focal points; each isolated group functions as a complete anecdotal entity within the larger scene.

Today we are properly skeptical of the subject matter—the depiction of contented slaves in stereotyped pastimes being visited by their genteel mistress—but the scene finds its roots in European pictures of benevolent upper-class ladies visiting the sick, the poor, and the old. In Johnson's painting, however, the lady's presence is secondary; she is not a pivotal figure in a humanitarian drama. She functions, then, either as a pictorial foil to a sentimentalized scene of bucolic slaves or as an observer to a way of life that was seen as purer and more virtuous than her own. Indeed, the content of the painting is ambivalent, giving no indication of the interpretation Johnson intended us to have.

At the time *Life in the South* seemed to have pleased all groups. To Southerners, the painting appeared as an apologia for slavery with its depiction of happy, well-fed slaves. A few abolitionists saw in the crumbling architecture a symbol of the "system" in decay. Henry Tuckerman, in 1867, quoted one such critic:

How fitly do the dilapidated and decaying negro quarters typify the approaching destruction of the "system" that they serve to illustrate! And, in the picture before us, we have an illustration also of the "rose-water" side of the institution. Here all is fun and freedom. We behold the very reality that the enthusiastic devotees of slavery have so often painted with high-sounding words. And yet this dilapidation, unheeded and unchecked, tells us that the end is near.[27]

34

Doves. (1860). Pencil on paper, 10½ x 15 inches. Museum of Fine Arts, Boston, M. and M. Karolik Collection. This drawing is a study for *Mating,* which was exhibited at the National Academy of Design in 1860.

The Chimney Corner. 1863. Oil on paper board, 15½ x 13 inches. Munson-Williams-Proctor Institute, Utica, New York, gift of Edmund G. Munson, Jr., by exchange.

New England Kitchen. Circa 1863. Oil on paper board, 17 x 21¾ inches. Collection Mr. and Mrs. R. Philip Hanes, Jr.

The value of the painting for us is ultimately historical rather than aesthetic. It was Johnson's first important painting and the one that brought him to the attention of the art world and the public. It remains the gauge by which we measure his later artistic progress.

Elected as an Associate to the National Academy of Design in 1859, Johnson was expected to contribute a self-portrait plus another painting to the Academy's permanent collection. The self-portrait (frontispiece) shows a self-assured man of 35, fully conscious of his own powers. The other painting he presented is a small, modest study of a black boy seated in a doorway playing a homemade flute. The thin, transparent sienna underpainting blends with the shadows and the rude wooden threshold in which the boy sits. His white shirt contrasts sharply with the predominating brown tones and sets off the active fingers of the young flutist. The realism is direct; details have been suppressed for the exigencies of the real subject, which is the total absorption of this youth in his music. The painting is private and personal, very different in content and form from the bustling panorama of *Life in the South.*

Johnson painted both black and white people in his paintings of home virtues in the early 1860s, combining and transposing various motifs. *The Chimney Corner* depicts a black man reading in the shelter of the fireplace. (The setting itself comes from a previous study, *New England Kitchen.*) Johnson incorporated this motif, of a man at the hearth, into *Sunday Morning* of 1866 (New-York Historical Society), but transformed the black man into a white grandfatherly type who reads the Bible to a room full of family members of all ages.[28] Such moralizing paintings of Bible reading by the hearth were as popular in Johnson's mid-century America as those of Jean Baptiste Greuze were in late eigtheenth-century France. Upon such homely virtues, it was declared, rested the stability of family life and the very morality of a nation.

In 1866 Johnson painted another work with an explicit moral, *Fiddling His Way,* which depicts a young black man earning his livelihood by entertaining a rustic family with his fiddle. The subject of the painting refers back to the country fiddlers of Mount (recall *Rustic Dance After a Sleigh Ride* of 1830, Museum of Fine Arts, Boston, and *Dancing on the Barn Floor* of 1831, Suffolk Museum and Carriage House, Stony Brook) and ultimately claims its heritage in the genre work of the Dutch and the early nineteenth-century English painter David Wilkie. In the Johnson work, however, the fiddler is dignified and serious; the spectators listen with awe and respect rather than amusement. The scene takes place in a shallow room peopled with illuminated foreground figures who contrast with dim figures enveloped in background shadows. As in *Life in the South,* the carefully composed scene contains multiple points of interest; groups exist independently but relate to each other through a glance or a gesture. The careful and conservative finish of the painting characterizes all Johnson's important exhibition pieces, and this picture went to Paris to hang in the United States section of the Paris Universal Exposition of 1867.

Heralded as the artist who could paint the American scene with honesty and freshness, Johnson during the 1860s searched for untried but relevant American subjects and sought ways to bring new life to older themes. Among the new subjects were events drawn from his experiences following the Union troops during the Civil War, when he sought out subjects that had at least a trace of sentiment, that would be acceptable in any parlor. He tried, however, to choose incidents that had actually occurred. *The Ride for Liberty,* of about 1862, depicting a slave family on horseback galloping full rein to the border and freedom,

Negro Youth. 1863. Pencil on paper, 8½ x 9¾ inches. Private collection. Photograph courtesy Hirschl and Adler Galleries.

was an incident he had witnessed at Centerville on the morning of McClellan's advance to Manassas on March 2, 1862.

War was also, to Johnson, a redirection of domestic concerns and occupations, and he gravitated to anecdotal scenes of the home front, such as *News from the Front,* 1861 (whereabouts unknown), depicting a woman and a young girl listening to a bandaged Union courier, or *Writing to Father,* 1863 (Museum of Fine Arts, Boston), in which the young child struggles to compose a letter for his soldier father, or *Knitting for the Soldiers,* 1861 (New-York Historical Society) in which a young girl knits busily for the troops. Life in the camps themselves, the endless boredom of the waits between battles, and the games and the reckless risks to combat that boredom were subjects better left to the more ironic vision of Winslow Homer.

Johnson did not stay with the troops throughout the war. He also turned his attention to the peaceful aspects of rural life and painted farmers at work and at leisure. In choosing scenes of rural white America he was following in the tradition of Francis William Edmonds, George H. Durrie, Tompkins H. Matteson, and William Sidney Mount—a tradition popularized by the prints of Currier and Ives. Indeed, Johnson's earliest dated work of rural life, *Corn Husking,* was engraved and distributed by Currier and Ives in 1860. But Johnson brought greater sophistication to this vein of Americana. His figures are not the country bumpkins found in many of the paintings of David Gilmor Blythe, James Goodwyn Clonney, Albertus D. O. Browere, George H. Durrie, and T. H. Matteson, but are dignified country people engaged in chores on their own farms. The quiet humanity of his rural subjects, the lack of grimaces and exaggerated gestures, appealed to most American collectors of mid-century, many of them wholly self-made men who looked back to their farm origins with nostalgia.[29] In fact, the absence of a condescending attitude toward his subjects distinguishes Johnson's paintings after 1860 from the European tradition of "genre rustique," a tradition predicated on the patrons' "superior" social standing—patrons who looked down at their social "inferiors" with detached amusement. The specificity of locale and the explicit individuality of the figures also distinguishes Johnson's genre paintings from his French contemporaries Jean-François Millet, Narcisse Diaz, Charles Emile Jacque, and Jules Breton, who themselves had eliminated caricature but had left their peasant figures as *types.* Johnson's approach of eliminating exaggeration but retaining individualization not only endeared him to a nation of democrats, but also set the precedent for the realism of Eakins.

The setting of *Corn Husking* with the open barn door parallel to the picture plane, and the motif of the dog, is reminiscent of Mount's barn interiors, such as *Dance of the Haymakers* of 1845. But in style *Corn Husking* shows a considerable advance in technique over Mount. The oil painting methods used by Mount and the older New York genre painters had usually involved the overall application of small, buttery strokes, with little regard for differentiating textural surfaces or for gradations of light in semi-enclosed spaces. In Johnson's painting, however, the atmosphere of dim light in the interior of the barn gradually and effectively brightens into sunlight at the doorway. The contrast between dark and light is expertly rendered by use of thin, transparent sienna shadows from which vague figures emerge in the background interior to the freely brushed, bright, dry strokes of unmixed color representing the rough cornhusks lying on the ground in front.

Corn Husking. 1860. Oil on canvas, 26 x 30 inches. Everson Museum of Art, Syracuse, New York, gift of the Hon. Andrew D. White, 1919. This painting was published as a lithograph by Currier & Ives in 1861.

Fiddling His Way. 1866. Oil on canvas, 23½ x 35½ inches sight. Coe Kerr Gallery, Inc., New York.

A Ride for Liberty—The Fugitive Slaves. Circa 1862. Oil on academy board, 21¾ x 26¼ inches. The Brooklyn Museum, gift of Miss Gwendolyn O. L. Conkling. There are two other versions of this painting, one of which is inscribed verso: "A veritable incident in the Civil War, seen by myself at Centerville on the morning of McClellan's advance to Manassas. March 2, 1862. Eastman Johnson."

The Letter Home. 1867. Oil on paper board, 23 x 27½ inches. Museum of Fine Arts, Boston, gift of Maxim Karolik. The original title, when the work was exhibited at the National Academy of Design in 1868, was *The Field Hospital.*

Card Playing at Fryeburg. Circa 1861-1866. Oil on canvas, 18⅞ x 29⅛ inches. Kennedy Galleries, Inc., New York.

Party in the Maple Sugar Camp. Circa 1861-1866. Oil on canvas, 30 x 40 inches. Hirschl and Adler Galleries, New York.

Study of a Negro Woman. (1862). Oil on canvas, 12 x 9½ inches. Collection of Kenneth Lux, Hamilton Gallery, New York. This is a study for a painting titled *Babe with Maid,* dated 1862.

Head of a Negro Man. Circa 1868. Oil on paper board, 19¼ x 15 inches. Collection of Mr. and Mrs. H. John Heinz III.

Barn scenes were ideally suited for showing outdoor light and dim shadowy interiors, and Johnson returned to such settings frequently. The subject of his painting *The Horse Trade* refers to Mount's paintings *Coming to the Point* (New York Public Library) and *Bargaining for a Horse* (New-York Historical Society). But again, the handling of transparent shadows, the strong triangular shape of the two men in the center, and the assured, loose brushstrokes of the foreground indicate a painter trained in the latest European academic techniques. Indeed, some of the subjects chosen, such as *Winnowing Grain,* remind one of the paintings of the same subject by Courbet and Millet. Johnson also showed men at rest— reading a newspaper, taking a drink, or lighting a pipe. Children, too, were represented helping with the chores, as in *Nest Hunting.* Taken as a whole, Johnson's pictures represent the cooperative aspects of farm life: all hands work no matter how young or old.

In the spring months of the early and mid-1860s, Johnson visited the maple sugar camps in Fryeburg, Maine, where he sketched scenes of the workers tapping the trees and boiling down the sap to make syrup. Here was an American subject that had several precedents in American art. N. Currier had published A. F. Tait's *American Forest Scene—Maple Sugaring* in 1855, and T. H. Matteson in 1845 had painted a scene of city people visiting rustics in a maple sugar camp. Johnson, however, seems to have had ambitions to paint a large panorama of the scene for which he painted many studies. He painted single figures and small groups and also experimented with various combinations of groups. *Measurement and Contemplation* and *Making Maple Sugar* depict men at work; *At the Camp—Spinning Yarns and Whittling, The Story Teller of the Camp,* and *Card Playing at Fryeburg* reveal the gayer aspects of merrymaking, of work, and of watching the syrup kettle. The largest of these studies indicates that Johnson contemplated quite a large composition. The emphasis of the oil sketches and studies is on characterizing individual figures, indicating local color, such as the clothing of the participants, and orchestrating color harmonies such as the red fire under the boiling syrup kettle juxtaposed against the gray spring skies and smoke-filled forest.

In 1868 Johnson painted *Boyhood of Lincoln,* a painting widely acclaimed when exhibited for the first time at the National Academy of Design Annual Exhibition in the spring of 1868, and of which Johnson made several copies. Sentiment about Lincoln ran high after his death, and representations of aspects of his life were popular in the late 1860s. With the gift for sensing subjects of topical interest, Johnson produced a painting combining several elements that virtually insured its success: it represented a healthy youth in a rustic setting, it represented Lincoln, and it represented the popular legend of Lincoln's homespun education out of borrowed books.

Boyhood of Lincoln. 1868. Oil on canvas, 46 x 37 inches. The University of Michigan Museum of Art. Johnson did smaller versions of this painting: one pastel drawing is in the collection of Berea College, Kentucky; a small oil on paper board is in a private collection.

In art historical terms, the importance of the painting lies in the fact that it brought history painting in America to the intimate and humanizing scale of genre. It depicted the nation's hero in the homely environment of his youth, acting out the moral drilled into every schoolboy, that in America hard work and perseverance would surely lead one to political or economic success. This essential content of the painting is underscored by the forms within the painting; the figure is braced against the rustic, shadowed background that dominates the space and threatens to envelop him; the face basks in the reflected glow of the fire and the book, a literal shining example for the youth of the nation.

Johnson was well known in New York and well liked by painters. He counted as his close friends not only George Hall and Worthington Whittredge but also Sanford Gifford and Jervis McEntee, landscapists who spent the summer months in the Catskills sketching nature. During the 1860s Johnson visited them there and painted several landscapes. The quiet naturalism of virgin woods or the grandiloquence of panoramic mountain and sky scenes were not subjects that appealed to Johnson as art; thus the few landscapes he did tend to be small in scale and infused with domestic sentiment.

At the Camp—Spinning Yarns and Whittling. Circa 1861-1866. Oil on paper board, 19 x 23 inches. Edward Speelman Ltd., London.

Lunch at Camp. Circa 1861-1866. Oil on paper board, 16 x 26¼ inches. Private collection. Photograph courtesy of Hirschl and Adler Galleries.

The Story Teller of the Camp (Maple Sugar Camp). Circa 1861-1866. Oil on canvas, 22¾ x 26¾ inches. Reynolda House, Winston-Salem, North Carolina.

The Woodcutter's Lunch. Late 1860s. Oil on paper board, 13¼ x 10⅝ inches. Collection of *Forbes* Magazine.

Woodcutter. Circa 1868. Oil on canvas, 21 x 17 inches. Smith College Museum of Art.

Harvest. Late 1860s–1870s. Oil on paper board, 6¼ x 17 inches. Collection of Mr. and Mrs. James W. Draper.

William Sydney Mount. *Dance of the Haymakers*. 1845. Oil on canvas, 25 x 30 inches. Melville Collection, Suffolk Museum & Carriage House, Stony Brook, Long Island.

The Horse Trade (Whittling in the Barn). 1866. Oil on paper board, 16½ x 21¼ inches. Deer-field Academy, The Charles P. Russell Collection.

Nest Hunting. 1864. Oil on paper board, 15 x 12½ inches sight. Collection of Edward Van Volkenburgh Sands.

Winnowing Grain. Late 1860s–1870s. Oil on composition board, 15½ x 13 inches. Museum of Fine Arts, Boston, bequest of Martha C. Karolik.

The Little Convalescent. Circa 1872-1880. Oil on paper board, 12¾ x 11 inches. Museum of Fine Arts, Boston, Frederick Brown Fund.

Woman Picking Waterlilies. 1865. Oil on academy board, 18½ x 15¼ inches. Private collection, New York.

Evening Newspaper. 1863. Oil on paper board, 17 x 14½ inches. The Herbert
W. Plimpton Collection, Amherst College.

N. Currier lithograph after A. F. Tait, *American Forest Scene—Maple Sugaring*. 1855. Photograph courtesy Kennedy Galleries, Inc.

Tompkins H. Matteson. *Sugaring Off*. 1845. Oil on canvas, 30¼ x 41½ inches. Museum of Art, Carnegie Institute, Pittsburgh.

Catching the Bee. 1872. Oil on canvas, 22 x 13¾ inches. The Newark Museum.

Not at Home. Circa 1872-1880. Oil on academy board, 26½ x 22¼ inches. The Brooklyn Museum, gift of Miss Gwendolyn O. L. Conkling.

Measurement and Contemplation. Circa 1861-1866. Oil on paper board, 20 x 24 inches. Museum of Fine Arts, Boston, bequest of Martha C. Karolik.

Making Maple Sugar. Circa 1861-1866. Oil on paper board, 12⅞ x 22⅛ inches. Collection of Mr. and Mrs. H. John Heinz III.

Sugaring Off. Circa 1861-1866. Oil on canvas, 52⅜ x 96 inches. Museum of Art, Rhode Island School of Design.

A Different Sugaring Off. Circa 1861-1866. Oil on canvas, 17 x 32 inches. Private collection, New York.

Sugaring Off. Circa 1861-1866. Oil on canvas, 34 x 54¼ inches. Collection of Mr. and Mrs. James W. Titelman. Photograph courtesy Kennedy Galleries, Inc., New York. The 1907 Sale Catalogue entry includes the following note: "The artist, in executing this as well as the foregoing study for the large picture, had a house built on wheels and provided with a stove, so he was able to move his temporary studio and work in comfort, and in this way make accurate and careful studies of all details of the sugar camp. For five years in the early sixties he spent three months of each year in the maple groves at Fryeburg, Maine, and in the summer seasons of these years sought his subjects on the battlefields of the Civil War...."

On Their Way to the Camp. 1873. Oil on academy board, 19¼ x 29⅝ inches. Collection of Mr. and Mrs. Clyde M. Newhouse. This work, dated 1873, was probably painted from sketches done circa 1861-1866. Johnson frequently painted and dated pictures years after he had made the original sketches.

The Catskill Mill. Late 1860s. Oil on paper board, 15⅞ x 22 inches. Collection of Mrs. Hulbert Taft.

The Boy Lincoln Reading. (1868). Charcoal and crayon on paper, 14⅞ x 12¾ inches. The Detroit Institute of Arts, gift of John S. Newberry, Jr.

In June 1869 Johnson married Elizabeth Buckley of Troy, New York, and the following summer he and his wife went to Nantucket for the season. Johnson responded enthusiastically to Nantucket, which seemed to be filled with characters and activities that appealed to him, and the couple returned to the island each summer.

One of the first large compositions done in Nantucket was *The Old Stage Coach,* based on a subject that Johnson had seen in the Catskills a previous summer. Here children are frolicking about an abandoned stagecoach on a bright summer day. They have thrown aside their school books and lunch pails and have plunged into the fanciful play of childhood, mimicking horses, grown-up drivers, and ladylike passengers. Around the bend come two more children hurrying to join the fun. The painting is unabashedly anecdotal,

The Quaint Old Village. Circa 1870-1871. Oil on paper board, 13 x 22¼ inches. Collection of Mrs. Hulbert Taft.

and it is not surprising that it proved to be immensely popular when it was exhibited at the National Academy of Design Annual of 1871.[30] Children were greatly sentimentalized in nineteenth-century art and literature, whether saintly Little Evas or naughty Tom Sawyers. The charms of childhood were especially praised by a self-conscious America, a country that defined its self-image in terms used typically to describe children: youthful energy, unconventional daring, unspoiled naiveté, and moral goodness. This sentimentality can also be understood as having a practical aspect: healthy children were one of America's prized national products to be nurtured carefully in order to swell the ranks of its future citizenry.

Study for The Old Stage Coach. (1871). Oil on canvas, 13¾ x 18 inches. Collection of Mrs. John Wintersteen. Photograph courtesy of the Philadelphia Museum of Art.

The Old Stage Coach. 1871. Oil on canvas, 36¼ x 60⅛ inches. Layton Art Gallery Collection, Milwaukee Art Center.

Johnson made a preliminary oil sketch, *Study for the Old Stage Coach,* that is quite new to his oeuvre, but indicates his awareness of current styles in painting. The sketch differs from the earlier sugaring-off sketches in its brighter tone, its broader and flatter areas, and its sharp oppositions of light and shadow. In composing such a sketch, in which the emphasis is so clearly on the organization of light and shadow, Johnson may have been reverting to the precepts of his old teacher, Thomas Couture, whose book *Méthode et entretiens d'atelier,* published in 1867, was at the time making a deep impression on American students. As an aid to the finished work, Couture had advised, one must first make a sketch of one's initial impression, laying in the places of the lightest lights and the darkest darks so that later the other tints and shades can be skillfully blended into the composition. Couture was, of course, following oil-sketch conventions used by sixteenth-century Venetians and modified over the centuries by other academic theoreticians; his contribution was that he codified the rules for nineteenth-century Frenchmen and Americans.[31]

Study for The Wounded Drummer Boy. (1871). Oil on paper board, 26 x 22 inches. Collection of Mrs. McCook Knox. There are two other oil studies for *The Wounded Drummer Boy* in the collections of the Fine Arts Gallery of San Diego and The Brooklyn Museum, as well as a drawing in the collection of The Century Association, New York.

The Wounded Drummer Boy. 1871. Oil on canvas, 47¾ x 38½ inches. The Union League Club. Photograph courtesy of the Frick Art Reference Library.

To our eyes, conditioned by the freedom of late twentieth-century painting, *Study for the Old Stage Coach,* with its bold, flat strokes, is more appealing than the finished work, with its emphasis on detail and anecdote.

We have evidence that Johnson, too, was fond of such first sketches and was reluctant to part with them. But it was the finished studio painting that he considered the exhibitable work of art.

The Impressionists in Europe, meanwhile, regarded such summary paintings of dark tones contrasting with light tints as final works. To a post-Manet generation these first bold direct impressions were more *real*—more analogous to our perceptions of the world—than were the contrived studio works. And *realism,* to a growing number of nineteenth-century men and women influenced by Balzac, Flaubert, and Zola and by Courbet and Manet, was the only viable attitude in a world where idealism, with its gods, heroes, and moral and aesthetic hierarchies, seemed bankrupt.

But Johnson and American artists of his generation were not thinking such thoughts. Johnson's generation had struggled too long and too hard to master *art* to be concerned as to whether that *art* was relevant to changing cultural attitudes in Europe. Johnson could privately like the sketches, as combinations of shapes and colors and as mementoes of his first impressions, but not as definitive statements. His apparent eclecticism of style can thus be understood, like that of other academic artists of the period, as comprising a sketch style and a finished style; and he maintained, in attitude, a rigid separation between them.

The same contrast between free, bold sketch and fastidiously detailed finished work is to be found in *Study for the Wounded Drummer Boy* and *The Wounded Drummer Boy.* In the finished work, exhibited in the National Academy of Design Annual Exhibition of 1872, Johnson reverted to the Civil War, choosing from the many stories made popular by history and literature of young drummer boys whose brave valor had inspired courage in their older comrades. Here the child, wounded but valiant and held aloft by a foot soldier, drums to raise the morale of the troops. The charming pathos of the subject disarms any genuine concern for the hardships of war or the pitiful condition of this child-warrior.

We find Johnson in the early 1870s brightening his palette and allowing light to play a more dominant role: both symbolically and structurally. He was also broadening and developing his themes at this time. Scenes of women—singly, in groups, or with children—figure in many of his paintings after 1870. As might be expected for the time, many of the women are cast in domestic or decorative settings and assume the roles dictated by their middle-class culture and environment: in the nursery tending a sick child, in the kitchen watching pots or comforting a baby, in a parlor playing with a child, or in a garden picking flowers.

The subject and the sentiment of *Mother and Child* of 1869 depicting a mother rocking a baby in her arms is not unusual. Nor is the lighting from the fireplace that gives a soft, even glow to this secular image of tender maternity. More inventive in its sentiment and in its use of light to underscore that sentiment is *The Peep,* dated 1872, when Johnson's own baby daughter Ethel would have been about the same age as the toddler here. In a middle-class Victorian setting, the two figures unite as a triangular shape, the apex of which is the glowing halo of blond baby hair backlighted by the sunshine pouring in through the window

Mother and Child. 1869. Oil on paper board, 14⅞ x 12¼ inches. Collection of Mrs. Walter Beinecke, Jr.

The Peep. 1872. Oil on paper board, 22 x 25 inches. Hirschl and Adler Galleries, New York.

at the right. Light, therefore, heightens the mood, and few nineteenth-century paintings represent more skillfully the joys of childhood or the charms of maternal indulgence.

Scenes of women in a decorative garden setting include *Woman Picking Waterlilies* of 1865, *Catching the Bee* of 1872, and *Hollyhocks* of 1876. In subject matter, though not in style, all three paintings have analogies with contemporary French painting of garden scenes (recall Claude Monet's *Women in a Garden* of 1866–1867, Musée du Louvre).

The three paintings of Johnson mark steps in his progression toward brighter light and stronger oppositions of light and shadow, a direction that Homer was independently taking at this time. But further analysis of the paintings reveals the fundamental difference between Johnson and Homer. In almost all of Johnson's paintings the figure is painted more carefully than his or her surroundings, even in *Woman Picking Waterlilies* where the face, because of its downcast position, is not personalized. In the highly keyed painting *Catching the Bee,* a painting exhibited at the National Academy of Design in 1873, the face of the young woman is cast in a softening shadow that sets her apart from the bright flowers surrounding her. The treatment of the forms in *Hollyhocks* ranges from the carefully painted soft feminine faces of the foreground figures to all objects in sunlight and finally to the summary treatment of the figures emerging from the shadows of the arbor. In Homer's paintings, however, such as *Croquet Scene* of 1866 and *Sunlight and Shadow* of 1872 (Cooper-Hewitt Museum, New York), there is no such distinction among the forms; all parts of the painting are treated equally.

It seems, in the characteristics that many of their paintings began to share (brighter key and flatter contrasts of light and dark), that Johnson and Homer were responding to the same trends[32] of the time rather than directly influencing one another. One cannot imagine that either would have naturally gravitated to the other. Although they both had studios in the University Building throughout most of the 1860s and they shared a common geographical heritage, New England, Johnson was, after all, twelve years Homer's senior.[33] Their personalities differed considerably. They approached their art, moreover, from totally different perspectives. Johnson began as a portrait draftsman, whose income therefore depended on his ability to render a suitable or pleasing likeness of the human face. He spent six years in Europe learning and perfecting an academic technique. His handling of light and color and composition were always balanced and planned and grounded in the academic rules of the day.

Homer began as a free-lance illustrator, describing actions and scenes as rapidly as possible. Accordingly, he concentrated on the total scene and on the total figure as it gives accent to the scene, simplifying line and mass so that they could be quickly read by the viewer. Portrait painting—the examination and interpretation of the human face—had no appeal to Homer.

It is Johnson's sketches, such as *On the Hillside,* not the finished works, that come closest to the look of Homer's paintings. But Johnson's sketches, with their simplified masses, contrasts of light and dark, and free brushwork, were never meant to be exhibited as independent paintings. When Johnson worked on a painting to bring it beyond the sketch stage, the human face became the object of his attention. (Note, for example, the careful finish of the face of the figure in *Woman on a Hill* as opposed to the sketchy treatment of the rest of the figure.) Even in his less finished pictures, there is a roundness to the faces absent in the

Hollyhocks. 1876. Oil on canvas, 25 x 31 inches. The New Britain Museum of American Art, Harriet Russell Stanley Fund.

Winslow Homer. *Croquet Scene.* 1866. Oil on canvas, 15⅞ x 26 inches. The Art Institute of Chicago.

Woman on a Hill. Circa 1875-1880. Oil on academy board, 25½ x 21¼ inches. Addison Gallery of American Art, Phillips Academy, Andover, Massachusetts.

On the Hillside. Circa 1875-1880. Oil on paper board, 15½ x 21¾ inches. Private collection. Photograph courtesy of the Frick Art Reference Library.

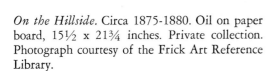

other parts of the painting. To Johnson there was a priority of values, the most important of which was the human face and its individuality. Homer, on the other hand, generalizes the faces of his figures. To Homer, and to a growing number of naturalists, the individualized human figure was only one element—even if perhaps the most interesting element—in a world indifferent to human needs.[34] Late nineteenth-century naturalism, and this includes Impressionism, involved not merely a change of subject matter (scenes of everyday life of the members of one's own class in which anecdote had been eliminated), but a philosophical attitude that turns away from hierarchical considerations and confers equal status on all *things*. To painters bringing this viewpoint to their art, all objects, shapes, and forms must exist equally on the canvas and be given equal treatment. (Moreover, moralizing or storytelling which depends for its effect upon visual and psychological focal points, that is priorities, had no place in such naturalist paintings.) But Johnson's paintings are wholly alien to this new philosophy and it is doubtful whether he would even have understood such radical trends.

In the 1870s Johnson painted several interiors of girls and women alone, engaged in private personal activities—removed from the company of men and children. In many of these, light acts as an accent to the mood or to symbolize the presence of an outside agent. In *Interesting News* light from the window softly radiates across the painting and illuminates the quiet activity of the young girl reading the newspaper. In

Interesting News. 1872. Oil on panel, 17½ x 22 inches. Private collection, La Jolla, California.

The Earring. 1873. Oil on academy board, 26 x 22 inches. The Corcoran Gallery of Art, gift of Capt. A. S. Hickey, U.S.N. (ret.), in memory of his wife, Caryl Crawford Hickey.

mood, in subject, and in the choice of its details—the map on the wall, the flower pot on the windowsill— it is reminiscent of the hushed interiors of Vermeer. This quiet, private light also pervades *The Earring,* in which the subject is caught at the moment of fastening an earring—a small moment but one requiring her total absorption. In *Not at Home* the light shining through the parlor suggests the movement of the woman who flees up the darkened stairs. In this painting, as in many seventeenth-century Dutch interiors, there is a suggestion of other rooms, of spaces beyond the confines of the canvas.

More pensive and inscrutable is the young woman in *Day Dreams* who gazes out the window at the falling snow. In this painting, one is tempted to see the window as a symbol of a world beyond the kitchen,

83

The Quiet Hour. Circa 1877-1878. Oil on canvas, 19 x 21½ inches. Collection of Mrs. J. Pierre Bernard.

In the Hayloft. Circa 1877-1878. Oil on canvas, 27 x 33 inches. The Fine Arts Gallery of San Diego, gift of Mrs. Herbert S. Darlington, 1935.

Barn Swallows. 1878. Oil on canvas, 27⅛ x 22¼ inches. Philadelphia Museum of Art.

Child Teaching Rabbit. (1878). Oil on paper board, 19⅞ x 15⅝ inches. Collection of Mrs. J. Pierre Bernard.

the sewing room, and the nursery, inaccessible to the young woman. But even if the window does not function as a metaphor, it functions as it always has in European art, as a transmitter of outside light into the interior.

In the late 1870s Johnson returned to barn scenes, the perfect setting in which to juxtapose luminous brown shadows with sunshine-struck highlights. Visiting his sister, Harriet May, who with her husband and children summered in Kennebunkport, Maine, Johnson found the occasion to paint his own daughter, the May children, and assorted neighbors in a series of barn interiors done in 1877 and 1878. The barn's cross-beam and its support break the composition of these paintings into rectangular units which suggest a more modern sense of design—especially in *Barn Swallows* and *In the Hayloft.* Yet, in the finished versions, such as *The Confab* (Wadsworth Atheneum) and *Barn Swallows,* Johnson could not resist an old-fashioned

86

picturesque touch here and there, such as a yellow hat against the green hay, or a bouquet of flowers on the crossbeam.

But the majority of his genre scenes were now located specifically in Nantucket, a place that was identified in the art public's mind with Johnson. "The man and the place," one critic wrote in the mid-eighties, "have a natural sympathy for each other. He is a chronicler of a phase of our national life which is fast passing away."[35] On the island he did a variety of landscapes as well as several interiors. In *Corn-husking Bee,* which was included in the International Exhibition held in Philadelphia in 1876, he returned to an earlier theme. But instead of limiting himself to the circumscribed barn interior of 1860, he opened the scene to the panoramic outdoors wherein brushstrokes are loose and open and touches of pure color are distributed throughout as lively accents to the brown and golden tones.

From the mid- to late 1870s Johnson made sketches and studies of cranberry pickers on the island of Nantucket. Cranberry picking, like the making of maple sugar, was uniquely American. The subject of workers picking berries in the fields had appealed to many American painters. Johnson may have seen Winslow Homer's *The Strawberry Patch,* which was illustrated in *Our Young Folks* of July 1868, or

Sheet of sketches. Circa 1872-1880. Pencil with touches of red and white on paper, 11¾ x 18¼ inches. Addison Gallery of American Art, Phillips Academy, Andover, Massachusetts.

Study for Corn Husking. (1876). Pencil and watercolor on paper, 18¾ x 12¼ inches. Free Library of Philadelphia.

Corn Husking. (1876). Oil on canvas, 27⅝ x 54½ inches. The Metropolitan Museum of Art, Rogers Fund, 1907.

Berry Picking. Circa 1875-1880. Pencil, watercolor, and Chinese white on paper, 7¾ x 19⅜ inches. Addison Gallery of American Art, Phillips Academy, Andover, Massachusetts.

Sketch for *Cranberry Pickers*. Circa 1875-1880. Oil on paper board, 13⅜ x 22⅝ inches. Kennedy Galleries, Inc., New York.

Opposite: *Cornhusking Bee*. 1876. Oil on canvas, 31½ x 50 inches. The Art Institute of Chicago.

Gathering Berries, illustrated in *Harper's Weekly* of July 11, 1874, although an equally viable source of inspiration could have been the numerous European paintings of similar themes. Millet had painted several versions of *The Gleaners,* many of which had found their way to our side of the Atlantic, as had paintings of rural workers by other Barbizon painters and their contemporaries: Charles Emile Jacque, Jules Dupré, Constant Troyon, and Jules Breton, among others. Such rural themes were, to be sure, a manifestation of the cultural protest against the industrial revolution with its concomitant overcrowded city slums, its urban pollution and human exploitation. And both Johnson and the Barbizon painters were caught up in this reaction to and escape from industrial realities. But the Barbizon painters, especially Millet, responded with a fatalism amounting at times to despair. The poor and anonymous peasants of Millet were venerated as the last surviving species from a time in which human labor had nobility and dignity.[36] Johnson did not so much react against urban realities as he ignored their very existence. To Johnson there were no poor people in America; his figures are middle-class Yankees working effortlessly and gaily, joking and flirting as they move from bog to bog in the autumn afternoon sun. He was, moreover, praised for just such an attitude. William Walton said:

...He...preaches no ugly gospel of discontent, as does so much of the contemporary French and Flemish art of this genre; his Nantucket neighbors know nothing of the *protestation douloureuse de la race asservie à la glèbe;* there is no *cri de la terre* arising from his cranberry marshes or his hay-stuffed barns.[37]

Indeed, it is Johnson's optimism and his celebration of the joys of rural labor—a labor in which the distinctions between working class and middle class were blurred—that endeared him to a generation. Much of his appeal and his "Americanness" for his own generation, as well as ours, lies in his nostalgic vision of an essentially classless society involved in American tasks.

Only a few of Johnson's many preparatory studies of cranberry pickers are illustrated here. The Addison drawing *Berry Picking,* probably an early study, contains color notations and notes of additional details. The *Sketch for Cranberry Pickers* adumbrates the extent and relative scale of the setting and the color tonalities of the harvest fields. The bulk of the studies, however, fall into two groups; those related to Yale's unfinished version and those related to the dated *The Cranberry Harvest.* The scene of the Yale painting incorporates the motif of the man emptying berries into a sack at the right. The motif also exists in two earlier versions in the collection of Mr. and Mrs. Clyde M. Newhouse and in a private collection. It is not known whether Johnson ever completed or planned to complete a painting based on the Yale study. He did finish another version, the dated *The Cranberry Harvest,* mentioned above, a painting that was rediscovered in England only within the last couple of years. In this painting, and the studies relating to it, the dominating motif is the standing, profiled woman who rises above the other workers as she looks to the right toward the horizon. This very motif may well have been borrowed from Jules Breton's *Les Sarcleuses,* a painting done in 1860 and exhibited at the Paris Universal Exposition of 1867. A second version of the Breton painting, dated 1868, was owned in the 1880s by Henry Probasco, a prominent Cincinnati collector. It was

Day Dreams. 1877. Oil on paper board, 23½ x 11¾ inches sight. Private collection, New York. Another version of this painting was sold at the 1907 Sale of the Works of Eastman Johnson conducted by the American Art Galleries, No. 102.

The Conversation. Circa 1875-1880. Oil on paper board, 22½ x 26½ inches. Addison Gallery of American Art, Phillips Academy, Andover, Massachusetts.

94

Cranberry Pickers. Circa 1875-1880. Oil on paper board, 19 x 29 inches. Collection of Mr. and Mrs. Ross M. Newhouse.

Cranberry Pickers. Circa 1875-1880. Oil on paper board, 22¾ x 27 inches. Private collection, New York.

The Cranberry Harvest. 1880. Oil on canvas, 27 x 55 inches. Vose Galleries of Boston, Inc.

Cranberry Pickers. Circa 1875-1880. Oil on canvas, 27 x 54⅛ inches. Yale University Art Gallery, bequest of Christian A. Zabriskie.

In the Fields. Circa 1875-1880. Oil on academy board, 17¾ x 27½ inches. The Detroit Institute of Arts, Dexter M. Ferry, Jr., Fund.

The Hatch Family. 1871. Oil on canvas, 48 x 73⅜ inches. The Metropolitan Museum of Art, gift of Frederic H. Hatch, 1926.

not unlikely that Johnson may have seen or known about the Breton painting. At the time comparisons were made between Johnson and Breton. S. G. W. Benjamin, in praising Johnson's *Cornhusking Bee* of 1876 (after having praised *The Cranberry Harvest* of 1880), had said: "In tone and colour and in the acute perception of rural human nature it loses nothing by comparison with the work of Jules Breton."[38]

In the Fields is a closeup study of the standing woman with several younger companions. As in the oil study for *The Old Stage Coach* the strong lateral light shatters the forms into adjacent shapes of light and shadow. The Arizona State version places the woman in a larger setting and eliminates two of her companions. The next version, in a private collection, adds many more figures and motifs: the mule and cart in the distance, the motif of the man seated in a chair, and the figures moving down into the forward center section of the painting. In the finished version the standing woman has become a dominant vertical axis among many verticals. In the Breton, on the other hand, the woman rises above the bent and anonymous bodies of her fellow peasants and is the solitary axis profiled against the evening sky. In each, the form and composition reveals a fundamentally different content: the content of the Breton is the awesome and solemn but necessary labor of the French peasant; the content of the Johnson is the democratic and even hedonistic gaiety of a Nantucket cranberry harvest.

The cranberry picking scenes represent the last paintings that Johnson undertook as a series. He also turned his attention in the late 1870s and early 1880s to interiors, using Nantucket people as models. He especially favored the old sea captains such as Captain Myrick, Captain Coleman, and Captain Manter. Captain Myrick, a picturesque bewhiskered gentleman who wore a stovepipe hat, seems to have been Johnson's favorite. One of the earliest paintings in which he appears is as a spry old man gesturing in *Nantucket Sea Captain* of 1873, placed in a rustic kitchen and surrounded by props, such as the painted brick mantel, the Windsor chair, irons and candlesticks, which were used repeatedly in other interiors (compare *The New Bonnet*). Captain Myrick figures as a leading character in other paintings, such as *A Glass with the Squire* (Ann Mary Brown Memorial, Brown University), and *The Reprimand* (whereabouts unknown), and is even found among the cast of *The Cranberry Harvest*.

Johnson's last dated genre work, *The Nantucket School of Philosophy* of 1887, depicting old men reminiscing of days gone by, is, in a sense, a group portrait scaled down to genre proportions. Such male camaraderie appealed to Johnson. His own image in his later years was one of a gregarious, portly, Victorian gentleman inclined toward group male fellowship. He belonged to almost all the artists' organizations in New York City, served on many fair commissions and government committees dealing with the arts, and frequented several men's clubs, where he was known for his good spirits and conviviality.

Johnson's last genre work exhibited at the National Academy of Design was *Embers* in 1899. In this painting the bent old man (again Captain Myrick) seated by the dying coals of the fire is himself an ember of a bygone era. The subject is especially appropriate for a concluding work, and one is tempted to fashion an analogy between the figure and Johnson, who himself was seventy-five years old in 1899.

By 1880 a new generation of painters led by Frank Duveneck, William Merritt Chase, and John Singer Sargent were painting different subjects in a different style. The old intimate and anecdotal nature of genre pictures was gone; the subjects which had seemed so picturesque were fading.

Cranberry Pickers in Nantucket (Study for *The Cranberry Harvest*). Circa 1875-1880. Oil, 26½ x 43½ inches. Oliver B. James Collection of American Art, University Art Collections, Arizona State University, Tempe, Arizona.

Jules Breton. *Les Sarcleuses.* 1868. Oil on canvas, 28½ x 50¼ inches. The Metropolitan Museum of Art, bequest of Collis P. Huntington, 1925.

Cranberry Pickers (Study for *The Cranberry Harvest*). Circa 1875-1880. Oil on canvas, 19 x 44 inches. Private collection. Photograph courtesy of Kennedy Galleries, Inc., New York.

The Blodgett Family. 1864. Oil on canvas, 30 x 25 inches.
Collection of Mr. and Mrs. Stephen W. Blodgett.

LATER PORTRAITS

After 1880 Johnson turned to portraiture almost exclusively. He had, to be sure, never given up his interest in making portraits. In the group portraits, such as *The Blodgett Family* and *The Hatch Family,* he combined portraiture and genre, placing the people he was representing in their own milieu. Such paintings as these, traditionally called "conversation pieces," trace their pedigree to England and seventeenth-century Holland. They are commissioned group portraits of wealthy patrons as they want to be seen, usually surrounded by sumptuous furnishings and a coterie of family and friends. In *The Blodgett Family* the time chosen as the occasion of the scene was Christmas and the holiday decorations and toys offered a set of natural props for the figures. The boy with his stick puppet provides a psychological focal point for this portrait of family harmony.

Mrs. Hatch. (1871). Charcoal heightened with white on paper, 8¾ x 9 inches. Private collection. This is a study for one of the figures in *The Hatch Family*.

Mrs. Ruggles. (1871). Charcoal and pencil heightened with white on paper, 9⅞ x 7⅞ inches. Private collection. This is another study for one of the figures in *The Hatch Family*.

Captain Nathan H. Manter. Circa 1880. Oil on canvas, 13 x 10 inches. Collection of W. Myron Owen.

Nantucket Sea Captain. 1873. Oil on canvas, 19¾ x 12½ inches. Collection of Mrs. Walter Beinecke, Jr.

For *The Hatch Family* Johnson executed very careful studies before combining them into a large and detailed tableau. Unlike the earlier group portrait, the figures in *The Hatch Family* spread out in panoramic array; the painting unfolds with a variety of detail within the red velvet and mahogany sitting room. It is, in a sense, the American scene indoors: a magnificent homage to the growing prosperity of the mercantile class of the post-Civil War years.

Johnson's portraits of himself and his friends are among the best he painted. That of Sanford Gifford, a much-loved friend of many artists, was done in 1880, the year that Gifford died. Indeed, the portrait may be a posthumous one; the expression on Gifford's face reveals an urgency and poignancy that suggests impending tragedy. The *Portrait of Edwina Booth,* the daughter of Johnson's friend Edwin Booth, is one of Johnson's most beautiful female portraits, with its delicate facial tints and clean, firm, outlined profile. The

The New Bonnet. 1876. Oil on paper board, 20¾ x 27 inches. The Metropolitan Museum of Art, bequest of Collis P. Huntington, 1925.

Captain Charles Myrick (Study for *The Reprimand*). (1880). Charcoal on paper, 10¾ x 6¾ inches. Free Library of Philadelphia.

Study for The Nantucket School of Philosophy. (1887). Oil on canvas, 22³⁄₁₆ x 27⅜ inches. Milwaukee Art Center Collection.

108

The Nantucket School of Philosophy. 1887. Oil on panel, 23¼ x 31¾ inches. The Walters Art Gallery, Baltimore.

Self-Portrait. 1899. Oil on canvas, 56 x 42½ inches. Collection of Mr. and Mrs. Patrick Coffey. In 1899, Johnson painted himself in the costume he wore to a "Twelfth Night" party held at The Century Club.

From our vantage point, a century after he approached the height of his influence, Johnson's career seems firmly established in the mainstream of American art. When he returned from Europe he was more advanced technically than any older American genre painter. The luminosity of his shadows, the care with which he drew and filled in his figures, the judicious deployment of forms and colors in a composition, the freedom of his final touches to give the impression of effortlessness, were technical marvels in the early 1860s. He covered a broad range of subject matter, not only including scenes of rural work and relaxation, as Mount had done, but also adding to the repertory of American painting such scenes as corn husking bees and cranberry picking.[38]

Up to Johnson's time genre painting in America had tended to patronize its subject matter, to follow established conventions in depicting the amusing and quaint ways of country yokels. In his best paintings Johnson eliminated comic faces and exaggerated gesture, traditional to genre painting, but he still individualized the figures. He presented scenes of everyday life that related to the lives of the people for whom he painted. His patrons, in the 1860s and 1870s, responded not with superior amusement over the antics of the "lower classes" but with a deep personal recognition of their own hardworking rural origins. Johnson depicted the myth—and myth is the collective fantasy of a nation—that hard work was not only virtuous but joyful. To a young nation struggling to become a major power this idealization of the working farmer and pioneer was, we can see now, a national necessity.

But the quarter century after the Civil War is also known to us as a sentimental age. Given Johnson's temperament, which blended so well with the sentimental character of his time, it is not surprising that he had a predilection for tender maternal scenes, for rosy-cheeked and adorable (if unreal) children, and for quaint old men.

Today we see Johnson as a painter who brought more sophisticated techniques to America, who extended the range of "American" subjects, often transplanting traditional European themes, and who brought a more dignified and democratic content to genre painting. He spoke to and for his own generation, and he was a great influence on a number of genre painters such as Thomas Waterman Wood, J. G. Brown, Thomas Hovenden, George C. Lambdin, and others. But he also lived through a time of transition, not always adjusting to the new philosophical and aesthetic attitudes of the late century, not always probing his own responses. He was perfectly capable of producing anecdotal and sentimental pictures while simultaneously experimenting with a lighter palette, looser brushwork, and summary treatment of forms. Indeed, Johnson's oeuvre marks the transition that took place in American art from the circumscribed and provincial style of Edmonds and Matteson to the open, painterly style of Duveneck and Chase, from the nativist subject matter of Bingham and Mount to the themes of self in the paintings of Homer and Eakins. Seen thus in the broader context of American art, it is the work of Eastman Johnson that forges the strongest link between the genre painting of mid-century and the realism of the late century.

Notes

1. William Walton, "Eastman Johnson, Painter." *Scribner's Magazine* XL (1906), 265.

2. *Ibid.*

3. Ralph Waldo Emerson, "The American Scholar [an address delivered before the Phi Beta Kappa Society, Cambridge, August 31, 1837]." *The Works of Ralph Waldo Emerson,* Edited by J. E. Cabot (Boston and New York, 1883), I, 113.

4. *Op. Cit.* "The Poet," III, 40–41 [first written in 1842].

5. The American Art-Union was founded as a non-profit organization by a number of businessmen in 1839 and was called during its early years of operation the Apollo Association for the Promotion of the Fine Arts in the United States. The stated aims of the organization were "cultivating the talent of artists" and "promoting the popular taste." To this end it bought paintings from American artists, which it distributed by lottery to its subscribers (in 1849 it distributed 1,010 works of art among 18,960 subscribers). In addition, it issued one or two engravings each year to all its members and an illustrated periodical from April 1848 through December 1851. As the result of legal actions brought against it, the American Art-Union folded in 1853. See Charles E. Baker, "The American Art-Union" in Bartlett Cowdrey, *The American Academy of Fine Arts and American Art-Union* (2 vols., New York: The New-York Historical Society, 1953), I, pp. 95-240. See also E. M. Bloch, "The American Art-Union's Downfall," *The New-York Historical Society Quarterly* XXXVII (1953), 331–359.

6. New-York Historical Society (American Art-Union—Letters to Artists), Letter from Andrew Warner to George H. Hall, dated June 8, [1849].

7. New-York Historical Society (American Art-Union—Letters from Artists), Letter from George H. Hall to Andrew Warner, dated July 24, 1849.

8. Mrs. Barbara Groseclose, after researching the archives at Düsseldorf in the summer of 1971, has informed me that the records do not include Johnson's name with those who were formally enrolled in the Royal Academy. In the Brooklyn Museum, however, this writer has seen a large sketch book of Johnson's, the cover of which is inscribed: "E. Johnson/ Royal Academy of Düsseldorf/Anatomical Class. /1849," which would indicate his attendance in at least one class at the Royal Academy.

9. New-York Historical Society (American Art-Union—Letters from Artists). Letter from Eastman Johnson to Andrew Warner, dated October 10, 1850.

10. New-York Historical Society (American Art-Union—Letters from Artists). Letter from Eastman Johnson to Andrew Warner, dated January 16, 1851.

11. Elsewhere the author is publishing her findings on the Leutze/Johnson collaboration on the engraver's replica of *Washington Crossing the Delaware,* a painting in the collection of Ambassador and Mrs. J. William Middendorf II. See also John K. Howat,

"Washington Crossing the Delaware," *The Metropolitan Museum of Art Bulletin* XXVI, No. 7 (March 1968), 289–299, and Raymond L. Stehle, "Washington Crossing the Delaware," *Pennsylvania History* XXXI (July 1964), 268–294.

12. New-York Historical Society (American Art-Union—Letters from Artists). Letter from Eastman Johnson to Andrew Warner, dated November 20, 1851.

13. Walton, *Op. cit.,* p. 268.

14. *Ibid.*

15. *Ibid.*

16. It is not known whether the works illustrated here were the versions exhibited at the National Academy of Design in 1856.

17. A representative remark by a critic is found in *The Cosmopolitan Art Journal* (June 1857) I, 118: "The hour has arrived when the necessities of our country not only justify, but inexorably demand, the production of a series of national paintings...." The artist Worthington Whittredge wrote in his *Autobiography* of the pressures to produce "American works" when he returned from Europe in the early 1860s: "I knew well enough that if I was to succeed I must produce something new and which might claim to be inspired by my home surroundings." "The Autobiography of Worthington Whittredge." Edited by John I. H. Baur, *Brooklyn Museum Journal* II (1942), 42.

18. James Thomas Flexner, *That Wilder Image* (New York: Bonanza Books, 1962), p. 78.

19. Roy Harvey Pearce, *The Savages of America: A Study of the Indian and the Idea of Civilization* (Baltimore: The Johns Hopkins Press, Revised Edition, 1965), p. 192.

20. *The Crayon* III (January 1856), 28.

21. Henry T. Tuckerman, *Book of the Artists* (New York: G. P. Putman & Son, 1867), p. 470.

22. Johnson never did much with these sketches, and they remained in his possession until his death. In 1909 his widow sold them to Richard T. Crane, Sr., a wealthy Chicago manufacturer, who purchased them expressly to give to the City of Duluth. Since 1929 they have been in the custody of the St. Louis County Historical Society of Duluth.

23. Originally exhibited at the National Academy of Design as *Negro Life at the South*, by 1867 it was called *Old Kentucky Home*, the title having been borrowed from Stephen Foster's popular song.

24. "National Academy Exhibition," *The Cosmopolitan Art Journal* III (June 1859), 134.

25. Anon, *The Crayon* (June 1859), 189.

26. *Ibid.,* p. 191.

27. Tuckerman, *Op. cit.,* p. 468.

28. For another instance of Johnson's racial transpositions, compare *Preparing Breakfast* (reproduced, *Antiques* LXXIII [March 1958], 223) with *Morning on the Farm* (reproduced, undocumented clipping, New York Public Library, Artist's File).

29. Luman Reed was one such patron. See Lillian B. Miller, *Patrons and Patriotism: The Encouragement of the Fine Arts in the United States, 1790–1860.* (Chicago: The University of Chicago Press, 1966), pp. 154ff.

30. One contemporary and effusive review is quoted in John I. H. Baur, *Eastman Johnson, 1824–1906: An American Genre Painter* (Brooklyn: Institute of Arts and Science, 1940), pp. 27–28.

31. Albert Boime discusses nineteenth-century attitudes in France regarding the sketch and the finished work in his *The Academy and French Painting in the Nineteenth Century* (London: Phaidon Publishers Inc., 1971). A discussion of the history of the sketch is to be found in *Masters of the Loaded Brush: Oil Sketches from Rubens to Tiepolo,* intro. by Rudolf Wittkower (New York: Trustees of Columbia University, 1967), pp. xv–xxv.

32. Other American artists were following a similar

1861–65	Followed the Union Troops on several campaigns during the early years of the Civil War. Spent the late winter months in Fryeburg, Maine, sketching outdoor scenes of the maple sugar camps.
1862	Joined the Century Club, New York City.
1868	Joined the Union League Club, New York City. Taught the fall term at the National Academy of Design.
1869	Taught the spring term at the National Academy of Design. Married Elizabeth Buckley of Troy, New York, on June 29. Vacationed in Murray Bay, Canada, during July.
1870	Only daughter, Ethel, born in May. Took his family to Nantucket for the summer.
1871	Bought property on Nantucket. Summered there for the rest of his active life. Painted his first dated outdoor Nantucket scene.
1872	Moved into 65 West 55th Street, New York City, where he kept a winter studio.
1875–80	Painted studies for the cranberry picking scenes during the summer months. Visited his sister Harriet May and her family in Kennebunkport, Maine, where he painted a series of barn interiors with children in 1877 and 1878.
1881	Began to paint fewer genre scenes, more portraits.
1885	Vacationed in Europe. Painted Grover Cleveland as President of the United States.
1887	Painted his last dated genre painting.
1891	Vacationed in Europe.
1895	Painted President Benjamin Harrison.
1897	Vacationed in Europe.
1906	Died April 5 in New York City.

Interior of Johnson's Studio. Originally reproduced in Edgar French, "An American Portrait Painter of Three Historical Epochs," *World's Work,* XIII (1906), p. 8317.

Selected Bibliography

A complete bibliography of works cited and consulted will be found in the author's doctoral dissertation, *The Genre Painting of Eastman Johnson: The Sources and Development of His Style and Themes,* nearing completion for the Institute of Fine Arts, New York University.

Ames, Kenneth. "Eastman Johnson: The Failure of a Successful Artist." *Art Journal* XXXIX, No. 2 (Winter 1969/70) : 174–83.

American Art Galleries. *Catalogue of Finished Pictures, Studies, and Drawings by the Late Eastman Johnson, N.A. to be Sold at Unrestricted Public Sale by Order of Mrs. Eastman Johnson at the American Art Galleries.* New York: American Art Galleries, 1907.

Baigell, Matthew. *A History of American Painting.* New York: Praeger Publishers, Inc., 1971.

Barker, Virgil. *American Painting: History and Interpretation.* New York: The Macmillan Company, 1950.

Baur, John I. H. *American Painting in the Nineteenth Century: Main Trends and Movements.* New York: Frederick A. Praeger, 1953.

————. *Eastman Johnson, 1824–1906: An American Genre Painter.* Brooklyn: Institute of Arts and Science, 1940. (Reprinted in 1969: Arno Press Inc.)

————. "Trends in American Painting, 1815–1865." *M. and M. Karolik Collection of American Paintings, 1815 to 1865.* Cambridge, Massachusetts: Harvard University Press, 1949.

Benjamin, S. G. W. "Eastman Johnson," *Some Modern Artists and Their Work.* Edited by Wilfrid Meynell. New York: Cassell & Company, 1883: 153–59.

————. "A Representative American." *Magazine of Art* V (November 1882) : 485–90.

Boime, Albert. *The Academy and French Painting in the Nineteenth Century.* London: Phaidon Press Ltd., 1971.

Brandon, William. *The American Heritage Book of Indians.* New York: American Heritage Publishing Co., Inc., 1961.

Craven, Wayne. *American Painting, 1857–1869.* Newark, Delaware: University of Delaware, 1962.

Crosby, Everett U. *Eastman Johnson on Nantucket: His Paintings and Sketches of Nantucket: People and Scenes.* Nantucket Island, Massachusetts: Privately Printed, 1944.

Flexner, James Thomas. *That Wilder Image: The Painting of America's Native School from Thomas Cole to Winslow Homer.* New York: Bonanza Books, 1962.

French, Edgar. "An American Portrait Painter of Three Historical Epochs." *World's Work* XIII (1906): 8307–8323.

Gardner, Albert Ten Eyck. *Winslow Homer, American*

Artist: His World and His Work. New York: Bramhall House, 1961.

Goodrich, Lloyd. *Winslow Homer.* New York: The Macmillan Company, 1944.

Grant, John B., Jr. "An Analysis of the Paintings and Drawings by Eastman Johnson at the St. Louis County Historical Society." Master's thesis, University of Minnesota, 1960.

Harris, Neil. *The Artist in American Society: The Formative Years, 1790–1860.* New York: George Braziller, Inc., 1966.

Hartman, Sadakichi. "Eastman Johnson: American Genre Painter." *International Studio* XXXIV (1908): 106–11.

Harvard University William Hayes Fogg Art Museum. *New England Genre: Art in New England.* Introduction by Museum Class. Cambridge, Massachusetts: Harvard University, 1939.

Hirschl, Norman. "Exhibition of Eastman Johnson—Forerunner of Homer and Eakins." New York: Frederic Frazier, Inc., 1937. (Mimeographed.)

Indiana University Art Museum. *The American Scene 1820–1900.* Introduction by Louis Hawes. Bloomington, Indiana: Indiana University Art Museum, 1970.

Jarves, James Jackson. *The Art-Idea.* Edited by Benjamin Rowland, Jr. Cambridge, Massachusetts: The Belknap Press of Harvard University Press, 1960. (First published in 1864.)

Keck, Sheldon. "A Use of Infra-Red Photography in the Study of Technique." *Technical Studies* IX (1941): 145–52.

King, Edward. "The Value of Nationalism in Art." *Monthly Illustrator* IV, No. 14 (June 1895): 265–68.

Larkin, Oliver W. *Art and Life in America.* New York: Rinehart & Company, Inc., 1949.

Low, Will H.; Beckwith, Carroll; Isham, Samuel; and Fowler, Frank. "The Field of Art: Eastman Johnson—His Life and Works." *Scribner's Magazine* XL (1906): 253–56.

Matthiessen, F. O. *American Renaissance: Art and Expression in the Age of Emerson and Whitman.* New York: Oxford University Press, Inc., 1941.

The Metropolitan Museum of Art. *19th Century America: Paintings and Sculpture.* Introduction by John K. Howat and John Wilmerding; texts by John K. Howat, Natalie Spassky, and others. New York: The Metropolitan Museum of Art, 1970.

Miller, Lillian B. *Patrons and Patriotism: The Encouragement of the Fine Arts in the United States, 1790–1860.* Chicago: The University of Chicago Press, 1966.

Neuhaus, Eugen. *The History and Ideals of American Art.* Stanford, California: Stanford University Press, 1931.

Pearce, Roy Harvey. *The Savages of America: A Study of the Indian and the Idea of Civilization.* Revised edition. Baltimore: The Johns Hopkins Press, 1965.

Richardson, E. P. *Painting in America: From 1502 to the Present.* New York: Thomas Y. Crowell Company, 1965.

Selby, Mark. "An American Painter: Eastman Johnson." *Putnam's Monthly* II, No. 5 (1907): 533–42.

Sheldon, G. W. *American Painters.* New York: D. Appleton and Company, 1879.

Spencer, Benjamin T. *The Quest for Nationality.* Syracuse: Syracuse University Press, 1957.

Tuckerman, Henry T. *Book of the Artists: American Artist Life, Comprising Biographical and Critical Sketches of American Artists, Preceded by an Historical Account of the Rise and Progress of Art in America.* 2 vols. New York: G. P. Putnam & Son, 1867. (Reprinted in 1967: New York, James F. Carr.)

Walton, William. "Eastman Johnson, Painter." *Scribner's Magazine* XL (1906): 263–74.

Whitney Museum of American Art. *Art of the United States, 1670–1966.* Text by Lloyd Goodrich. New York: Whitney Museum of American Art, 1966.

125

[Whittredge, Worthington]. "The Autobiography of Worthington Whittredge, 1820–1910." Edited by John I. H. Baur. *Brooklyn Museum Journal* II (1942): 7–68.

In addition, the author has drawn upon the resources of the Archives of the St. Louis County Historical Society, Duluth, Minnesota, and the unpublished letters of Eastman Johnson in the possession of his living relatives, the New York Public Library (Manuscript Division), the New-York Historical Society (American Art-Union—Letters from Artists), and the Archives of American Art.